Mustangs

ERIC ETHAN

Gareth Stevens Publishing
MILWAUKEE

For a free color catalog describing Gareth Stevens Publishing's list of high-quality books and multimedia programs, call 1-800-542-2595 (USA) or 1-800-461-9120 (Canada). Gareth Stevens Publishing's Fax: (414) 225-0377.
See our catalog, too, on the World Wide Web: http://gsinc.com

Library of Congress Cataloging-in-Publication Data

Ethan, Eric.
    Mustangs / by Eric Ethan.
      p. cm. — (Great American muscle cars—an imagination
  library series.
    Includes index.
    Summary: Surveys the history of the Mustang and its designs,
  engines, performance, and costs.
    ISBN 0-8368-1747-8 (lib. bdg.)
    1. Mustang automobile—Juvenile literature. [1. Mustang
  automobile.] I. Title. II. Series: Ethan, Eric. Great American
  muscle cars—an imagination library series.
  TL215.M8E84 1998
  629.222'2—dc21   97-41188

First published in North America in 1998 by
Gareth Stevens Publishing
1555 North RiverCenter Drive, Suite 201
Milwaukee, WI 53212 USA

This edition © 1998 by Gareth Stevens, Inc. Text by Eric Ethan. Photographs by Ron Kimball (cover, pages 5, 7, 15, and 17), Nicky Wright (pages 9, 19, and 21), and John Lamm (pages 11 and 13). Additional end matter © 1998 by Gareth Stevens, Inc.

Text: Eric Ethan
Page layout: Eric Ethan, Helene Feider
Cover design: Helene Feider
Series design: Shari Tikus

Printed in the United States of America

1 2 3 4 5 6 7 8 9 02 01 00 99 98

TABLE OF CONTENTS

Words that appear in the glossary are printed in **boldface** type the first time they occur in the text.

THE FIRST MUSTANGS

The Ford Mustang was the dream of a man named Lee Iacocca. He was employed by the Ford Motor Company, first as an engineer and later as a salesman. Many of his new-car customers were looking for an inexpensive, sporty-looking car like the Ford Thunderbird from the 1950s.

Beginning in 1961, Iacocca directed **design** work that led to the first Mustang **prototypes**. In mid-1964, the first Mustangs were shipped to car dealers.

Iacocca's dream was an immediate success. The Ford Mustang became the most popular American car of the 1960s.

*Muscle cars, such as Mustangs, are two-door sports **coupes** with powerful engines made for high-performance driving. Pictured is a Mustang from mid-1964.*

WHAT DID EARLY MUSTANGS LOOK LIKE?

The Mustang was a small car for its time. In the 1960s, most American cars were large and heavy **sedans**. The Mustang's short 90-inch (229-centimeter) **wheelbase** and lightweight construction made it a standout.

In the first years, Mustangs came in three body styles — hardtop, convertible, and fastback coupe. All three models shared a long hood and short rear deck. This design was so popular that it was often copied by other automakers. In honor of the Mustang's winning design, the term *Pony car* became common. Other Pony cars include the Chevrolet Camaro, Pontiac Firebird, and Plymouth Barracuda.

A long hood and short rear deck helped make Mustangs extremely popular. Shown is a 1966 Mustang convertible.

WHAT WAS THE FASTEST MUSTANG?

A basic Mustang came from Ford with a 200-cubic-inch (3.2-liter) or 280-cubic-inch (4.6-liter) engine. The greater the cubic inches, the more **horsepower** an engine can create. Horsepower means speed. Even the smaller 200-cubic-inch (3.2-liter) motor has the power of 271 horses.

Mustangs with bigger engines and certain **accessories** to improve the car's handling were also available. The Ford Motor Company worked with Carroll Shelby, a famous American race car driver, to design the Shelby GT-350 Mustang. In 1965, this car could be ordered with a 700-horsepower engine and other racing accessories. This car was fast enough to beat nearly every other car at official road races.

The 1968 Ford Mustang Shelby GT-500 KR was one of the fastest Mustangs ever made.

MUSTANG ENGINES

Shelby added special parts to Mustang engines to improve their power and performance. Pictured on the next page is a special Shelby modified Ford V8.

The air cleaner on top of the engine carries a special decal. It identifies the engine as a high-performance version of the Ford 289-cubic-inch (4.7-liter) engine. The air cleaner is open all the way around to allow air to flow more easily into the **carburetor** on which it sits.

The word *Cobra* on the silver valve cover further identifies the motor as a Shelby modified version. Only a small number of Shelby GT-350 Mustangs were made in 1965. Those that still have all their original parts are very valuable today.

A Shelby modified GT-350 motor in a 1965 Mustang.

MUSTANG INTERIORS

The 1965 GT-350 Mustang interior had many of the special features found on high-performance Shelby Mustangs. Seat belts were still rare in regular production cars in 1965. But this car had extra-wide seat belts with heavy-duty buckles. The belts were especially useful to Shelby modified GT-350 Mustang owners who took their cars to the racetrack to drive at top speed. Racing seat belts and other handling equipment added by Shelby made these Mustangs safer to race.

The Carroll Shelby Cobra logo is visible in the center of the steering wheel. Shelby's name can also be seen on the right of the dashboard. Extra **gauges** that told the driver how the engine was operating were added to the middle of the dashboard.

Interior of the 1965 GT-350 Mustang.

MUSTANG RACING

Some Mustangs straight from the factory could go very fast. But Shelby Mustangs with extra racing accessories were the cars that road racers wanted. The Shelby GT-350 came with many of the features that turned Mustangs into road rockets.

The engine in the GT-350 could produce nearly 400 horsepower. The tires were wider than those on most cars. All four wheels had **disc**-brakes to make the car easier to control. Heavy parts, like the steel gear box, were replaced with lighter ones. All these features made the GT-350 a trophy-winning road racer.

Shelby GT-350s, like this 1966 version, were built with racing in mind.

POPULAR MUSTANGS

The GT-500 Shelby Mustang shows the clean design and accessories that made it such an attractive car. This style is called a fastback. The roof line goes quite far toward the end of the trunk. Do you see the small Cobra logo just ahead of the door?

Most cars are purchased for practical transportation. But every once in a while, a design is so good that it becomes a great deal more. When Mustangs were first produced, there were more customers than cars. This took the Ford Motor Company by surprise. Many months passed before enough cars could be manufactured to meet the demand.

A beautifully maintained 1968 Shelby GT-500 fastback with special wheels.

THE LAST ORIGINAL MUSTANGS

The early 1970s marked the end of the line for the original Mustang body design. Bigger and faster motors were no longer produced. Around the same time, the rising price of gasoline and concerns about air **pollution** changed what people wanted in cars. Safety and **fuel economy** became important considerations.

Mustangs continue to be manufactured today. The Mustang pictured was built in 1995. It looks very different from the original models. Newer Mustangs use much less gas and are safer to drive because they are slower. But some people feel the newer models are not as exciting!

This compact Mustang made in 1995 still has the long hood and short rear deck that made the original models so popular.

WHAT DID THE ORIGINALS COST?

Iacocca wanted the Mustang to be an affordable car. Through the 1960s, a basic Mustang cost around $4,000. The special Shelby Mustangs cost under $7,000.

The simplest model of a car with no **options** is sold at a **base price**. The customer can then choose optional features, such as bucket seats, a bigger motor, and special tires. Each of these options adds to the total price. Many people like their car to be different from any other to reflect their personality. Carmakers know this and offer customers many different options.

The horsepower behind this 1964-1/2 Mustang convertible reveals why Ford Mustangs were called Pony cars.

WHAT DO MUSTANGS COST TODAY?

Today's new Mustangs cost more than twice the base price models of the 1960s. But that is nothing compared to the high value of the Mustangs built thirty years ago. The first 1964 models and all the Shelby versions are especially valuable.

Car collectors do a lot of work to **restore** and **preserve** their vehicles. A well-restored Shelby Mustang can easily cost ten times what it did when it was manufactured. Fortunately for car collectors, a large number of Mustangs were made. Buyers can usually find a 1964 or 1965 model.

GLOSSARY

accessories (ak-SESS-or-eze) — Objects that provide comfort or decoration.

base price (BASE prise) — The price of an object before options are added on.

carburetor (CAR-burr-ay-ter) — The part of a car that supplies the engine with an explosive, vaporized fuel-air mixture.

coupe (koop) — An enclosed, two-door automobile for usually two people that is normally smaller than a sedan.

design (dee-ZINE) — The plans and specifications for a new product.

disc (DISK) — A thin, flat, circular object.

fuel economy (FU-el ee-CON-oh-me) — A rating that reveals how far a vehicle can travel on a certain amount of gasoline or other fuel, and therefore its fuel efficiency.

gauge (gayj) — An instrument that indicates how well or how poorly a motor is operating.

horsepower (HORS pow-er) — A system for measuring engine ability based on the amount of weight one horse can pull.

option (OP-shun) — A feature that can be added over and above the regular features.

pollution (poh-LU-shun) — Wastes and poisons that enter the air, land, and water.

preserve (pre-ZERVE) — To keep intact and free of decay.

prototype (PRO-toe-type) — A model that is used as a guide to make copies.

restore (ree-STORE) — To fix an item so that it becomes like new.

sedan (seh-DAN) — A large, enclosed automobile that can seat six adults. It has a front and rear seat.

wheelbase (WEEL-base) — The distance between the front and rear axles of an automobile.

WEB SITES

www.globalxs.nl/home/e/ed/muhome.htm

www.mcmallenargus.com/pub/strperf/mustang

www.ford.com/

mgfx.com/mustang/

www.geocities.com/MotorCity/7356/mustang.html

PLACES TO WRITE

Mustangs & Fast Fords
McMullen and Argus Publishing
774 South Placentia Avenue
Placentia, CA 92870-6832

Mustang Illustrated
774 South Placentia Avenue
Placentia, CA 92870-6832

Shelby American Automobile Club
P. O. Box 788
Sharon, CT 06069
Fax: 860-364-0769

Mustang Club of America
3588 Highway 138, Suite 365
Stockbridge, GA 30281

INDEX

24